Shipping Container Homes

A Guide to Building Your Own Container Home

Tony Murdoch

Table of Contents

Introduction

Shipping containers are repurposed for a myriad of uses that add value and prolong the life of these widely used and readily available commodities. When a container becomes worn, damaged, or cannot be returned due to the unsustainability of shipping an empty container, instead of having it occupy space and be an unsightly obstruction or waste in a landfill, it can be transformed into a beautiful modern container home. Based on its size and the amount strewed globally, it would prove costly to dispose of; not just monetarily but also to the environment—to melt one container requires over 8000kWh!

Containers have long been used outside of their original intent of transporting goods; storage has been one of the leading roles served by shipping containers. In part, shipping containers were created to avoid the hassle of having to unload the goods being transported; instead, they are stored in the container until arriving at their final destination which in some cases may take months and a voyage over land and sea, moving from a ship, truck, and rail.

The first large-scale repurposing of shipping containers ever documented was in the Vietnam war, when containers used to transport goods were kept in the country and used by the military for storage and to create posts, living quarters, and command centers. The concept of shipping containers being used as a habitat first entered print in the 1970s with the thesis by college student Nicholas Lacey. However, the first steps in materializing the concept came some 17 years later when Phillip C. Clarke submitted a patent.

The concept of container homes would receive much thought through the years; however, the large-scale push needed to make its appeal mainstream would not arrive until after the start of the 21st century. This push, as with most, required an event that changed the landscape and made it necessary to adjust; this push came in the form of a global financial crisis.

The global financial recession of 2008 was the most significant economic downturn since the great depression of the 1930s. It affected multiple industries across continents. Real estate, in particular, took a significant hit. The average debt to Gross Domestic Product (GDP)—the amount of debt a country owes against the value of the goods or services it can produce annually—within the U.S. rose from an average of 46% at the turn of the century to a whopping 73% in 2008.

The US economy has long had a credit culture which has, for the most part, proven beneficial as it allows individuals and families to gain access to opportunities that had it not been for the ability to borrow the money needed in the present and pay it back at a later date, their goals would have been unattainable; mortgages for home purchases, car loans, student loans, credit for large and even small everyday purchases are a large part of what the American dream represents.

In this system, unfortunately, are many negatives that will arise; borrowing becomes so encouraged that oftentimes no account is placed on a person's ability to repay their debt should they encounter some financial turbulence. The borrowers would either reject reason or were ignorant of their inability to repay. Lenders were willing to take the risk, given that the interest on their loans could be paid. When the recession hit and customers had to default on their loans, the banking sector suffered irreconcilable losses. Had it not been for a massive government bailout, a crash of the industry would have been unavoidable.

Hard lessons had to be learned as the culture of extravagance was unsustainable and needed to be changed; the need for more than what was necessary stemmed from an idealism that more is better. Despite not requiring an excessive number of cars, houses, or jewelry—it is the American way to want more. Today's growing culture of compact living is a stark contrast, primarily centered around the financial benefits a minimalist lifestyle brings and a desire to stay off-grid away from the hustle and costs associated with living in a major city.

Changes in the economic landscape were joined by the realization that the consumerism that had long been the norm was becoming increasingly unsustainable; thus, a minimalist lifestyle became necessary for many in search of financial and environmental stability. The tiny house movement provided an option for not only millennials whose needs differed from the previous generations but also proved to be a viable option for retirees on a limited budget; allowing them to shed some of the costs associated with the lifestyle they had led over the years.

Millennials, contrary to prior generations that felt somewhat compelled to start a large family and buy a house with a white picket fence and a yard that could accommodate and nurture the family's growth, have begun to seek a lifestyle of less. The desires of a generation of baby boomers were motivated by a wish to have a seemingly better life after coming out of a great depression and a world war. There was also the status that living in a particular class neighborhood brought; albeit a facade in most instances, as maintaining such a lifestyle would often leave families stretched beyond their means.

The current cost of purchasing a home as well as its maintenance has driven the demand in the real estate market to a low; this has caused a downturn in the development of new properties and skyrocketed the cost of those available, which brings a need for alternatives to be sought not only by millennials but older retirees on a limited budget seeking options that not only save them money but also require less upkeep. One idea and the most cost-effective option was building a tiny home using repurposed shipping containers.

Many characteristics make a shipping container the ideal option for being repurposed as a home; the material used is durable and manufactured to withstand rusting and other decay, so exposure to the elements will not easily cause damage. It is made of steel and designed in such a way that thousands of pounds can be stacked on it. The structural integrity will remain sound. It offers ease of use, versatility in design, expansion, and stackability as shipping containers are built to a standard dimension.

Having decided that a shipping container home is ideal, then comes the task of creating the perfect home. There are several factors to take into account on the path to transforming a simple rectangular box into a space that is either modern or vintage in design and has all the standards, plus the luxury amenities that make a comfortable living space.

Before making any purchases, a detailed assessment should be made of the functionality the container home will need to offer; this is key in planning the location, size, design, and construction. Each step in the process of building a container home compliments the next; securing the site is imperative as it provides insight into the possible size; knowing the size home being built allows the design to start taking form, design provides a layout and an assessment of how construction will proceed, and construction has to be considered in all the previous steps in terms of both its limitations and potential.

The following questions will have a bearing on the steps that are needed and must be asked to obtain a clear objective. They are as follows:

- Location- Is there a desire to move off-grid, to a secluded area, or be closer to the city. Does the state or county permit container homes?

- Size- How many persons will the home accommodate daily, and are guest quarters required?

- Design- Will priority be placed on indoor or outdoor living? Are there any special features such as a balcony that should be included?

- Construction- What is the available budget? Will the project be DIY, a hired contractor, or a mixture of both?

This book will delve into each of these elements, providing readers with a step-by-step breakdown that will prepare them for each stage, ensuring that they have the knowledge to see their project through from start to finish. Being informed of the steps involved, what to expect, and how to steer clear of common mistakes will not only improve the likelihood of success but also the possibility of saving time and money.

Chapter 1: Location First

Once the land you intend to build on has been identified and ascertained, all the other elements can start to take form. A detailed and realistic assessment must be conducted to establish what needs to be done before the site can be worked on, for example:

- Does the lot need to be cleared, excavated, or fortified? Prepping the area may be necessary as there is likely an overgrowth of bushes and trees that need to be cut. The building site may also be on a slope that requires leveling the land itself, and it may need to be fortified to meet the code and qualify for a residential building permit.

- Are there any utilities such as water, electricity, or sewage lines? One of the most significant commonalities of persons who build a container or tiny home is a desire to get off the grid or move to an area not densely populated. Moving farther away from the populous has some downsides, as infrastructure that makes a home habitable will likely not be available; water, electricity, and sewage will often require additional efforts to implement but is entirely achievable. The options are as follows:

  - Water - rainwater harvesting is the ideal method; this depends on the conditions of the location.

Another option, although unlikely and may require a survey to be done if not readily available, is a natural underground catchment such as a well.

- Electricity - renewable energy has made great strides in recent times as many people, primarily millennials, are becoming more conscious of their carbon footprint and attempting to reduce the amount of fossil fuel they use. Most new homes, regardless of the type, are opting for renewable options such as solar energy; depending on the area's coverage from the sun, a house can run entirely on solar energy powering all its functions.

- Sewage - waste management is handled by the municipality in most populated areas; therefore, moving away from the coverage area poses a need that must be addressed. There are several options here, such as installing a sewage tank or by installing a composting toilet system.

- Is the area accessible by car or truck, or is it only accessible by boat? A paved roadway may not be available nor even a beaten path depending on how secluded the location is; in this case, the path may need to be cleared and a roller used to flatten the surface as the movement of material, equipment, not to mention the container is vital.

If the property is on an island that is not connected by roads and is only accessible by boat, that complicates things but is nonetheless surmountable. Ferries are likely available and can be used to haul the container, materials, and equipment.

- Does the state permit container homes? The zoning laws of your county can be found at the following offices: county courthouse, city hall, county recorder's office, or other city or county departments such as the tax assessor's office. An online search for the specific office based on your area is recommended.

- What building codes and permits are needed to qualify your structure as habitable? Shipping containers are not a conventional building material, as there isn't a lot of past recorded usage of this material in most states. The process of setting codes for its usage is relatively unknown; therefore, it can be difficult to get approval for building with this material. Special accommodations may need to be allotted for authorization to be granted, which in most cases will require an engineer approved by the county to work with you in stipulating what measures must be taken, and ordinances adhered to in order to have your container home building approved as habitable.

The container home project relies heavily on location selection; before any decision can be made, it has to be established where the container home will be located. The state or county it is intended to be in may have regulations preventing container homes from being built. Special permits may be required as well as requirements and guidelines that will change the entire course of construction to inhibit or require certain specifics to meet code.

Many container homes are built off-grid or in otherwise secluded areas that lack infrastructure such as electricity, water, and even a roadway. Based on the size and weight of a container, this may pose a problem as heavy-duty machinery is necessary in the transport and placing of the container on-site. In these events, steps must be taken to facilitate the required equipment, which means an additional cost is likely.

Knowing the location first allows for seamless planning of the other aspects; otherwise, your decisions are done blindly and would be based on speculations, not facts. Doing so will likely become detrimental to the project as mistakes will be made, which will result in a loss of time and money.

Permits, Building Codes, and Zoning Laws

Building a residential property is not as straightforward as having the desire and ability to afford it. There are requirements that must be met and guidelines that must be followed. Limitations on where certain types of housing can be constructed and the standards that must be met are a means of protecting homeowners and the interests of the wider community. Specifically, many of these standards pertain to disasters from both natural and human elements such as hurricanes, earthquakes, and fires.

Following the rules and guidelines when building a house has its benefits; firstly, if you decide to sell the house being built upon its completion or in the future, its value will be higher because you have followed the permits and building codes protocols. Attaining property insurance also depends on the contractor's adherence to the building requirements.

It cannot be stressed enough that you thoroughly research the zoning laws of your area, ensuring that the lot you intend to purchase is marked for residential use. Also, the building code should be used as a guide when planning and designing, and the requisite permits need to be attained. Failing to become educated or disregarding the necessary process will lead to delays in being approved.

Below are some of the things you must research for your particular area before planning your container home build:

- Permits - as the name suggests, permits are associated with gaining permission. Permits for residential developments fall under the categories of production homes and custom homes. Production homes are multiple houses built with the exact same specifications, usually by a developer, while custom homes are unique houses where a plan is drawn up for a single dwelling. One of the terms of obtaining a permit is being subject to mandatory inspections to ensure that the contractor is adhering to the terms of the permit; if the inspector locates a discrepancy, the contractor must have it rectified before the build can be completed. The submission of detailed drawings, which include the measurements, structural layout, floor plans, and the materials that the build will be comprised of, must also be submitted to have the construction permits approved.

    - The following are some of the main types of permits that must be obtained when building a shipping container home:

        - Residential building permits - applied for by the contractor or architect on the project. Obtaining this permit is mandatory for construction to proceed, and a detailed plan of the project must be submitted for the project to be approved.

- Electrical permits - obtaining the services of a licensed electrician is mandatory for the installation of wiring to pass building codes and be approved by inspectors.

- Plumbing permits - a licensed plumber's services are also required to install the piping for water and sewage for the construction project.

- Building codes - there are standardized building codes that must be adhered to by contractors, architects, and engineers. When constructing the structure of a house, these codes address the electrical system, plumbing system, fire safety, and HVAC of the home. Variance in climate and natural disasters each region is subject to determines what building codes are required in that state, city, or town. Confirmation of the required codes is the responsibility of the parties involved in the construction; the building codes for a specific area may be located on an online database, if not, inquiries can be made at the local building codes department in your area.

- Zoning laws - zoning laws regulate the purposes for which land may be used; certain areas are marked for specific types of usage. They are:

  - Residential - land used for housing, either single-family or multi-family units.

  - Recreational - these lands are reserved for recreational purposes; rural and urban areas have areas reserved for different activities. In rural areas, these activities include fishing, hunting, camping, and hiking. In urban areas, these activities include parks, biking, hiking trails, as well as jogging paths, and playing fields.

  - Agricultural - land used to grow crops and raise and farm animals. Agricultural land varies in the scale of farming that is allowed; in some cases, large-scale farming is permitted, and in others, it has to be limited to poultry or a small farm.

  - Commercial - land reserved for commerce such as the sale of goods and services; these areas are set aside to facilitate businesses such as shopping malls and plazas. An excellent example of a commercial district is

Rodeo Drive in California which is famous for having high-end stores.

- Industrial - land reserved exclusively for manufacturing, goods processing, and storage. Some industrial complexes include sawmills, oil refineries, and chemical plants.

- Transport - land that is used for private and public transportation of goods and people such as roadways, railroads, airports, and highways.

- Ordinance and covenants - These are rules specific to the neighborhood where the property is located. These rules serve to restrict extravagance in height and size when building or adding an extension, in order to keep a sort of uniformity of the properties in a community.

Projected Budget

Land purchase for the purpose of constructing a residential property has recently been at its highest rate since 2006 due to a shortage of homes available for sale. The disparity in supply and demand not only affects the availability but also has an impact on prices; this is a driving factor in encouraging new homeowners to purchase a lot of land and build a starter home, such as a shipping container home, at a fraction of the cost of buying a single-family home.

The price of land, similar to the price of a house, varies from state to state. Numerous factors account for the low or high cost of land designated for residential use, such as:

- Infrastructure - the level of amenities available in a specific area will influence the price of land in that area.

- Commute - despite the desire to move farther from populated areas becoming more common in recent times, areas that require a longer commute to get to a municipal zone, especially if an established system of transit does not exist, tend to lose value due to this shortcoming.

- Availability - as with other transactions, supply and demand are major deciding factors on prices. High demand with a low supply will result in a higher price for limited available land, and vice versa; low demand with a high supply will result in lower, more negotiable prices.

The top five highest average costs per acre of land by State are as follows: New Jersey ($196,410), Rhode Island ($133,730), Connecticut ($128,824), Massachusetts ($102,214), and Maryland ($75,429).

While the top five lowest costs per acre of land by the state are as follows; Montana ($2,283), South Dakota ($2,135), Nevada ($2,116), New Mexico ($1,931), and Wyoming ($1,558).

Chapter 2: Selecting the Ideal Size Shipping Container Home

Size does matter, at least when determining the size of your home. There are several factors to take into account when deciding what size home is suitable for you. As with traditional homes, assessing the number of persons being housed, what type of activities it will need to accommodate, and what the budget will allow, are questions that need to be answered.

Shipping containers are available in a range of sizes; the most common types are as follows:

1. 8ft x 20ft or 160 square feet or 14.85 square meters

2. 8ft x 40ft or 320 square feet or 29.73 square meters

3. 8ft x 45ft or 360 square feet or 33.45 square meters

4. 8ft x 48ft or 384 square feet or 35.67 square meters

5. 8ft x 53ft or 424 square feet or 39.39 square meters

The standard height of a container is 8ft (2.44m); however, anomalies exist with two types differing from the standard 8ft; they are; high cube, which is a slightly larger height of 9ft 6in (2.90m), and half-height which is noticeably smaller at the height of 4ft 3in (1.30m), however, the standard height of 8ft is predominantly used globally and therefore, is more readily available for purchase.

Assess the vital things that must be included when deciding on the size of the shipping container home. Also, the size of the lot must be taken into account, as well as the number of people it will house. Container home sizes may range from a single container, all the way up to a huge combination of containers creating a family home with two or more stories and encompassing multiple living spaces such as living and dining rooms.

The average bedroom size ranges from 132 to 144 square feet, which would be the bulk of the area in an 8 x 20 ft container leaving only about 28 to 16 square feet of additional space. Practical thinking in the design stage is imperative to ensure that the space is utilized as effectively as possible. Acknowledging the restraints based on size and coming up with solutions will test your level of creativity, but it has and can be done.

Most of the single container homes being built utilize an 8ft x 40ft container which offer 320 square feet of livable space; this is enough space to convert into a bedroom, a living area, kitchenette, and a bathroom. The design variations are many, and all depend on your preference; utilizing outdoor living in the design also provides additional space for daily activities.

Shipping containers are ideal as they are built to be stacked and have a standardized size so they can be fitted to align perfectly. While using a single container may meet the needs of some prospective shipping container homeowners, these will primarily be single people and young couples with no children. Others may be looking for more space to house a larger family or simply to have more rooms for amenities such as an office or a washroom. Stacking and aligning multiple containers offers a broader width for bigger rooms and multiple stories. The following are just a few of the variations possible when using multiple containers:

- Two 8ft x 40ft containers stacked one atop the other provides two stories of 640 square feet of space.

- Two 8ft x 40ft containers aligned side by side provide a 16ft wide space for much bigger rooms. Adding a bridge: a section between two or more aligned or staggered containers, a bridge is usually comprised of a roof and two walls at the front and back; this addition blends into the containers on either side and will add more open space and further broaden the width of the house. The frame on the sides of the containers facing each other will need to be removed for the open space; reinforcement then becomes necessary and extra material for columns will be essential to strengthen the structure.

- Four 8ft x 40 ft containers are aligned and stacked, with the house's opening either on the broad or narrow sides. Four 8ft x 40ft containers equate to at least 1,280 square feet, which can facilitate at least three bedrooms, two bathrooms, a kitchen, and a living area. Adding a two-story bridge on the narrow side opens the possibility for a massive two-story open floor plan.

- A combination of an 8ft x 40ft and an 8ft x 20ft container, either stacked or aligned, provides 460 square feet that offer a variety of possibilities not only in the type of rooms you would like to have them serve as but in how you wish to combine them; side by side or the broad side of 8ft x 40ft connected to the narrow side of 8ft x 20ft container, it all depends on the design you have in mind.

- Of note, having the containers attached is not mandatory; multiple containers can be sprawled across the property, offering differing living quarters and privacy in situations where they could be used as an Airbnb.

A single container home represents the ideals of many people who choose container living; it is minimalist and has a very low carbon footprint. The size also does not prevent the occupant from creating a comfortable, relaxing space that represents what they wish to have in a home. Creating an outdoor area that connects with the indoors adds more livable space and provides an opportunity to utilize the location's landscape.

Due to the modular nature of shipping containers, with planning and creativity, they can be transformed into whatever goal you had in mind for a home. While a single container home may prove sufficient for many, the choice will ultimately be determined by the size dwelling that the prospective homeowner wishes to build; they may decide to use either a single container or have multiple, either aligned or stacked.

Used vs. Brand New Containers

Shipping containers may be purchased when they are either brand new, have only had a single use, or have been used multiple times. The amount of usage a container undergoes will affect the cost and availability. The following is a brief breakdown for deciding what level of use is ideal when selecting a shipping container for building your home:

- Brand new - new containers may be purchased from a manufacturer or a dealer most likely located in the country of manufacture; these containers are not readily available unless you reside in the country they are manufactured. Buying a brand-new container is the most expensive option, particularly if they aren't manufactured locally.

- Single-use - this is the ideal choice for most people building a shipping container home; they are also more readily available. Most containers delivered to a location that doesn't deal in a lot of exports and is unable to send back goods will choose not to bear the cost of sending back an empty container to the source of origin, which results in containers being left idle. Single-use containers are also a good choice as they are less likely to suffer from the wear and tear of multiple uses and based on their availability, the cost will also be noticeably less for them to be acquired.

- Multi-use - these are containers that have been shipped more than once; while it is possible to get a container that has been used multiple times that is still in good condition, they are often in a less than ideal state. When purchasing your container, if you are able to locate a multi-use container in a satisfactory state, expect to pay less than you would for a brand new or single-use one.

Projected Budget

The cost of a shipping container is primarily based on its condition, size, and age. Other things are factored in, such as repair history, damages, the type of cargo, and the number of trips it has taken to transport cargo also determines how much a shipping container costs. The lifespan of a shipping container used to transport goods at sea is about 15 years, but this may be cut short. New shipping containers used for storage from the offset and kept from the damaging elements of sea freight may last up to 50 years.

The more economically sound choice and readily available are used containers, either 8' x 40' or 8' x 20'. The price of a container may range from $1,400 to $6000. The standard prices of used shipping containers are: 8' x 20' ($1,200-$2,500) and 8' x 40' ($2,600-$3,300), though this may vary based on your location.

The following are the standard prices to expect when purchasing a shipping container:

- New or single-use: $5,000 to $6,000
  - no visible damage, one-year-old, has only transported goods once; highest quality and durability

- Premium: $3,000 to $5,000
  - the highest grade for used containers, great condition, a minimal amount of damage; between two to eight years old

- Grade A: $1,900 to $2,500
  - certified as air and liquid-tight, a minimal amount of rust or damage, certified seaworthy; over eight years old

- Grade B: $1,500 and up
  - certified as air and liquid-tight, a fair amount of rust and damage, not certified seaworthy; over eight years

- Refurbished: $1,500 and up
  - used containers that had to be repaired; prices dependent on age and repair history

- As-is: $1,000 and up
  - purchase without verification of state or certificates of assurance, expect damages you are responsible for resolving

Chapter 3: Planning Essentials

The planning and design stage of building your shipping container home encompasses the architecture, layout, as well as indoor and outdoor design. There are tried and proven principles that may be used as a template for creating an aesthetically pleasing and comfortable layout and design. While these guidelines provide an outline for the configuration of your home, the choices you make must be based on your unique situation and personal preferences.

Container homes offer a wide range of design options; they are a blank canvas on which the prospective homeowner may allow their creativity to radiate. Depending on the homeowner's preferences, the design can be simple, cost-effective, and even rustic, or they may opt for elegant, high-end, and modern.

There are so many details to factor in that it may seem overwhelming to decide what layout and design are the right choices for your home. Start by determining the orientation of your container(s) based on where on the structure you intend to place the windows and doors and in which direction they should face. The utilization of the aesthetics the property offers is vital; the placement of the containers should be based on elements such as the views the property offers, the direction of the sunrise and sunset, the direction of the daylight, and airflow.

Heating, ventilation, and air conditioning (HVAC) guarantee occupants' comfort. Taking advantage of the elements such as sunlight and airflow to either subsidize or substitute is a smart choice and will result in savings on utility bills. Utilizing solar energy for heating and cooling is a widely used practice and has been tried and proven. There are limitations, of course, depending on the region's climate, seasonal changes, and weather; therefore, it's usually best to install a complete HVAC system.

The positioning of the building must be based on the geography of the area, such as terrain, landscape, climate, natural vegetation, water bodies, and soil. Position your balcony, windows, and doorways in order to make maximum use of the natural elements that the area provides. The key is to take advantage of the solar heating from the sun during colder months, and design and align windows in such a way as to keep the house cool in the warmer months. Landscaping is also an excellent method of providing shade for the home; palm trees are a perfect choice as they can be introduced close to maturity. In areas where the change in seasons is extreme, seasonal trees that bloom in the summer months will provide shade when the temperature is warmest and shed their leaves to allow sunlight to pass through during the winter months.

Windows should be on the southern side of the property for maximum usage of sunlight; however, it is understandable that this may sometimes lead to over-exposure during the peak hours, specifically noon when the sun is at its highest level in the sky. To combat this, the installation of sidings on the house to block out some of the sun's rays is a good idea. Installing blinds, curtains, or window shades is also an effective way of regulating the amount of sunlight entering the home; they also offer a privacy screen, especially for homes designed with wide open windows.

During the summer months, the sun sits higher in the sky, and the days are longer. These conditions will remain until the fall when the earth starts to rotate back to its regular axis and culminates in winter when the reverse occurs; the sun lowers in the sky and causes temperature drops and results in shorter days. The impact that the change in seasons will have on the sun's position and the climate is also a matter of great importance when positioning your home. The earth is constantly tilting as it rotates around the sun, which causes the southern and northern hemispheres at different intervals to experience changes in temperature, which causes the seasons. The use of shading devices is positioned so that in the warmer months, it blocks direct sunlight from entering the house, and in the colder months, when the position of the sun shifts, it is at an angle that allows sunlight to flow in more freely.

The sun rises in the east and sets in the west regardless of where on the planet you are located. There are slight variations throughout the year, but sunrise and sunset remain in the same general direction, either rising north-easterly or south-easterly or setting south-westerly or north-westerly, so it is safe to align your house based on this. For example, the bedroom can be placed in the direction of the sunrise or away from it. Building a balcony in the direction of the sunset can make a great addition.

Architecture and Layout

Hiring a trained architect is an invaluable investment in any construction project; a good architect will take into account all the factors that will go into the completion of the project. These include but are not limited to: confirming the customer's wishes, assessing the geography of the land, adherence to the zoning laws and building code for the area.

The architectural aspect of a construction project is complex, and it is vital that it is done right. For this reason, the hiring of a professional is the safest bet. However, with in-depth research into the required procedures and meticulous assessment of all the factors, someone with basic drawing, sketching, or 3D rendering skills may be able to contribute heavily to this process.

The planning aspect of building a shipping container home provides the opportunity for future homeowners to take their ideas, create a vision, and ultimately bring that vision through to fruition.

The planning process will determine the vital decisions for building your home; every detail must be thoroughly analyzed. There should be a measurement of all the areas throughout the house, as well as an account of the total distance of the property; a calculation of the length, width, and depth paired with determining the material being used will enable the creation of an accurate budget. Achieving this will not be an easy task; the process consists of multiple steps, none of which should be bypassed. The steps in the process are as follows:

- Consultation process - the homeowner will share their initial thoughts regarding the size of the dwelling, the utilization of the lot, additions such as a loft or deck, and the home's orientation (for example, the direction that the master bedroom faces). The architect will then take all of the homeowner's layout suggestions and conduct an in-depth survey or employ the services of a surveyor to ascertain whether the zoning laws, as well as the building codes that cover the area the lot is located, will facilitate their requests. Additionally, the size of the lot, the geography, the daylight, the wind stream, and the views the property offers will be taken into account to ensure maximum utilization of the features the property may offer.

- Schematic design process - rudimentary design ideas, typically 2-3 are drawn, sketched, or 3D renderings are created. These basic designs will explore the functionality as well as the possible aesthetic value that can be garnered. These designs are intended to materialize the possibilities available and are entirely malleable based on the homeowner's wishes; insight from the homeowner should be encouraged and aspects of the different designs may also be combined during this stage.

- Design development process - after the homeowner has agreed to all the major factors, the architect is now able to go to the drawing board and create a detailed plan. Meticulous details are included for all aspects of the foundation and the interior and exterior designs. The building starts to take a permanent form as the type of materials, and the functions of the home begin to take shape; types of doors, flooring, cooling/heating, furniture, positions of power outlets, and light fixtures all are included in order to ensure that every aspect of the home is laid down for the construction stage. These drawings will be in a layered form that illustrates the foundation finishes such as electrical wiring, plumbing, insulation, and HVAC as well as the visible finishes such as power outlets.

- Documentation process - there are two documents or rather master drawings that will result from the work an architect would have done on designing the building: the construction set and the permit set. The construction set remains on the building site and serves as a guide for the contractor, who must follow the details set forth by the architect in this plan to ensure that the site remains within the code set by the permit. The other document is the permit set submitted to local authorities for approval of the building site; the permitting office will review the proposed building plan, check for its compliance with zoning laws and building codes, and ensure that it is structurally viable. Approval of a requested permit can vary based on the size of the project; permits in areas under constant development where the architect utilizes the standard design schematics used in that area will be approved a lot quicker than a large-scale project or a project in an area that is protected such as a historic district.

- Contractor process - Having completed the task of laying out what the building will entail, then comes the task of actually constructing it; this is the stage that a contractor will come in to actually manage the day-to-day running of the construction. Some firms will not only provide an architect but will have staffed contractors who will take over after the architect has completed their part. The homeowner may also open a bid for contractors to submit their requests for the project or take over the contractor's role if they themselves are competent in construction. The architect will still be involved but only in a supervisory role to ensure that the plans they set for the building are being adhered to, and in the event that the contractor has a request to change a material the architect stipulated, then the approval of the architect is mandatory for any of those changes to be made. It is vital that all the plans set forth in the document created by the architect and approved by the local permitting office are adhered to by the contractor.

Indoor and Outdoor Design

The elements of design are as follows:

- Color - hue; light or dark, and intensity; bright or dull.

- Shape - either geometric shapes such as rectangles, circles, or organic shapes which are free-forming or naturally occurring shapes.

- Line - malleable in the sense that a line may be horizontal, vertical, diagonal, or curved. It may also vary in width, intervals, and density.

- Texture - the way a surface feels or the perception it provides of a feeling based on the visual texture.

- Direction - how a design guides the viewer; horizontal, vertical, or oblique.

The elements of design provide the material and, when paired with the principles of design, create the style needed to make a space more appealing and functional. Design principles may also be combined to improve their effectiveness. To gain an understanding of the design principles, let us delve into what they are:

- Unity - Combining the different design elements, each element should have a clear purpose in the design and complement rather than bombard the other.

- Movement- visual aids using the design elements to direct the viewers' eyes to the intended focal point.

- Contrast - this design principle utilizes extremes of a design element to emphasize, such as using one color as a background and then using text in the polar opposite color to convey a message. This may also be done using shapes, textures, direction, and so forth.

- Emphasis - purposefully allowing one aspect of a design to stand out in relation to the rest in order to help in ensuring its intended purpose is conveyed.

- Space - how the elements interact with the background they are placed on; having space around or within design elements can help to add emphasis.

- Alignment - elements are arranged, ordered, or aligned to create a visually pleasing connection.

- Repetition - combining elements to create association and consistency, which in turn strengthens a design.

- Continuation - the feel of expectancy that comes from having a pattern or a line extend.

- Perspective - the distance that the viewer perceives between elements.

- Proportion- the size of an element in relation to another; placing a more prominent element against a smaller one will emphasize the larger.

- Rhythm - the use of one or more elements repeatedly which gives a sense of regular or irregular organized movement.

- Pattern - the repetition of design elements, such as on a wallpaper.

- Variety - helps to keep a design interesting and may include a mix of design elements.

Having listed the elements and principles of design, we can now move on to how they are used in indoor and outdoor design to make a living space more functional and aesthetically pleasing. It is important to differentiate what is intended for outdoor vs. indoor use and how they can tie in together to create a functional space that has different elements and follows the principles of design.

Interior design needs differ from the exterior in many ways despite both sharing the same design elements and serving the same purpose of adding beauty and comfort to an area. The interior space would have furniture that shares a similar design; however, the material used for the indoor chair will not last as long if it were to be used on the exterior as the natural elements would cause wear at a much faster rate. Also, the doors begin to serve additional purposes for exterior uses versus interior uses; for the interior, a door is mainly to provide privacy and serve as a border between rooms, whereas exterior doors offer a level of security; therefore, exterior doors are built with more sturdy materials.

Container homes are often built on a smaller scale than other types of houses and outside of municipal areas with more of a rural landscape; therefore, it is often ideal to have the bulk of the living space outdoors. This makes creating a functional and aesthetically pleasing outdoor space vital. The majority of the exterior design is covered under landscaping which comprises the garden, deck, and patio area. Despite encompassing mainly natural elements, landscaping draws on the elements and principles of design that were explored earlier. Landscaping encompasses unity, form, line, color, texture, scale balance, emphasis, sequence, simplicity, and variety.

Furniture and Decor

The visual aspect of the home is arguably as important as the structural; having a stable house that will keep you safe and protected from the natural elements is important, but also is having a welcoming, calming, and pleasantly designed house that provides comfort and gives a feeling of serenity and joy. The choice of furniture can affect the available space, so it is best to choose with the amount of space available in mind. For larger areas, the grandness of traditional furniture and decor will give a plush and homely feel; however, that space will feel more open with sleek and clean contemporary or modern designs.

The color palette is also a deciding factor; for example, traditional designs are primarily brown and darker colors, and contemporary or modern designs utilize more sheen and glossy looks. The choices of furniture are a representation of the homeowner's taste, and the comfort and feel garnered differs with each person.

Interior design has gone through a myriad of phases through the centuries. Style and functionality are constantly evolving. While there have been mere fads that failed to withstand the test of time, there are also undeniably timeless trends that have been and will continue to be a staple in home decor. The following is a brief breakdown of the different design styles:

- Traditional - this design style has withstood the test of time, dating back to the era of England's Queen Victoria in the 19th century. The characteristics of a traditional design style are embellished dark woods, grand and intricate designs, expensive fabrics and textiles, as well as excessively cushioned furniture.

- Modern - the styles of the 20th century still have an impact today and are widely known as modern indoor designs. Characteristics of this style are the simple color palette; primarily white, black, and gray, as well as glossy materials.

- Contemporary - as the name suggests, contemporary design refers to the style of the present. As time passes, what is considered contemporary also changes. One of the characteristics of contemporary design style is the use of metal and glass as these materials have a sleek reflective surface.

- Transitional - a mix between the plush of traditional and sleek of contemporary. Characterized by the blend of furniture; rounded wooden designs of traditional design with the sleek metallic or glass of modern or contemporary designs.

The fundamental pieces of furniture that the interior must have, are beds, tables (dining and coffee), sofas, and chairs. Decor includes paintings, sculptures, mirrors, vases, and ornamental lighting. How each piece relates to each other will give the room its character; the architecture of the furniture, the color, and patterns and placements all play a role in transforming a room into a living space.

Projected Budget

Planning and design is the process of creating a vision that will guide the aesthetics of building your home. This provides direction and offers a footing for moving forward; therefore, it must be done correctly. The cost adds up as all the factors are taken into account; in addition to the fees for hiring an architect and a designer, the costs of furnishing and decorating an entire house will account for a large percentage of the budget for the entire shipping container home.

Securing the services of an architect should be the first priority. The cost for an architect's services will be dependent on the size of the property being designed, the complexity and detail of the design, the reputation/experience of the architect, and their required involvement and follow-ups. Another factor that affects the variation in the cost of hiring an architect is location; as with most services, the price fluctuates depending on the state.

Architects will charge either a flat fee, hourly rates, and in some instances, although an unlikely practice, per square foot. The average flat rate charged across the United States for basic architect services, which entail the drafting of a plan, is $5,000; this translates to a range of between $2,000 - $8,000. Depending on the level of the architect's skill and the amount of effort and follow-up exerted an architect may cost up to $40,000 in some cases. A skilled architect charges an hourly rate of between $125 per hour to $250 per hour, with the actual amount determined by the same factors used by architects charging a flat rate. In some rare instances, architects will charge per square foot for their services; in these cases, the rate is between $2 - $15 per square foot, and how much is charged is also determined by the same factors as the previously listed billing methods.

While not required as much as having a skilled architect, a designer will add invaluable input that will benefit the outcome of your shipping container home. Designers mainly charge an hourly rate along with miscellaneous fees for travel and making purchases on a customer's behalf. An interior designer will charge between $100 and $200 per hour for their services, which adds up to an average of $5,000 for designing an average home.

It is far more difficult to place a price on furniture and decor as there is not one set design style, and the elements included in a design plan will range in price based on innumerable factors. A traditional design will utilize all-natural wooden furnishing, which costs more than the typical factory-manufactured furniture associated with modern or contemporary design. The designer may even opt to include an antique piece that easily outvalues all other furnishings in that room, possibly all combined.

Let's explore the different elements that each room comprises as well as the average cost in an attempt to arrive at an estimate. The two primary living spaces in any home are the living room and bedroom; therefore, more effort is usually placed on ensuring that these particular rooms offer a sense of solace to their occupants.

The following are the furnishings that a typical bedroom will include, as well as an average price range:

- bedframe and mattress - $700 - $2,000

- nightstands - $180 - $300

- dresser - $400 - $800

The living room is of equal importance and must be treated as such when being designed. While the bedroom is a private getaway for inhabitants, the living room serves as a welcome for guests and affects the impression that is made on persons who may visit your home. Living room furniture and their average prices are as follows:

- sofa/couch - typically a 3-piece that includes an armchair and loveseat - $1,800 - $2,600

- accent chair - $850

- coffee table - $120 - $260

- carpets and rugs - $290 - $500

Chapter 4: The Construction Phase

All the manual tasks done throughout the project fall under construction. This stage is arguably the most important as it materializes all the visions and planning and spans the entire project length, from getting the land ready for work to installing finishes. Planning is essential to the construction phase, and how well the planning and design stage was executed will determine how smoothly the construction phase goes. A poorly thought-out plan will cause a lot of errors resulting in a loss of time and money.

By this stage, you will have hired a competent architect to create a concise design, or you may have pushed your boundaries and found yourself able to formulate a detailed and well-researched architectural plan that your local permit office has approved. Now, it is time to start the construction phase and watch your vision become a reality. Whether the decision was made to have the firm that created the architectural draft proceed with the construction phase, or have a new contractor come in, or even have the project be a DIY, it is imperative that the architectural plans are strictly adhered to during construction.

All the planning and assessment thus far will culminate in this most critical stage, construction. This is where the shipping container home will start to take form, from laying the foundation to installing finishes. The project's construction stage covers all the actual practical work that needs to be done and is, therefore, the most essential, time-consuming, and costly.

The construction process begins at the inception of the project; in most cases, the land has to undergo some level of clearing or excavation. There may also be a need to install enforcements in areas where the soil is not as dense; this is primarily done by creating ditches along the border of the areas that need to be enforced and filling them with concrete mix and steel supports. Once the lot has been deemed structurally strong enough to be built on, the foundation for the containers to be placed will follow.

Shipping container homes are an ideal choice for persons who intend to make the building of their home a Do It Yourself (DIY) project; the frame of the house is already constructed, and therefore there is little need for the workforce that a brick-and-mortar house would require. This does not mean that it is a simple task, as there are still guidelines and regulations that must be followed.

Shipping containers were created to keep the goods they transported safely from the elements in some of the most torrential conditions. A container in good working order is sealed, waterproof, and airtight; therefore, modifications must be made to the structure for it to become habitable. There are, however, some aspects of a building project which are mandated to have approved and licensed professionals complete and sign off. Also, it is imperative for DIY projects that plenty of effort be placed in becoming knowledgeable about the building codes, local land use codes, zoning laws, and required permits. Failing to submit the necessary documentation or not following the codes and laws governing building a home in your area may lead to having to cease construction and making costly adjustments, which will affect not only your budget but also the timeframe.

Step-by-Step Guide

The stages of construction vary based on the design set forth by the architect; some components are standard and are included in all architectural plans, and by extent the construction process. In addition to there being a set list of tasks that must be accomplished, there is a specific order in which these tasks should be done. The following is a brief overview of the standard steps taken during the construction process, listed in the order they are typically completed:

- Prepping the lot for construction - modifications to the land's topography may be necessary to make the lot a safe work site. Based on the intended positioning of the house on the lot, changes might also become necessary in that regard. Excavation is the likely method that will be used to achieve a level surface or to clear a path for access to the entryway and the rest of the property. The foundation of the lot may also require strengthening in order to facilitate the additional weight of the structure being placed.

- Building the foundation - a solid foundation erected on stable ground is essential to ensure your house remains level and is not affected by the soil sinking or shifting under the weight of the house. The foundation is also responsible for elevating the container off the moist ground, thus protecting it from corrosion. There are multiple types of foundations to choose from; however, the main types are:

  o pier foundation - a popular choice due to it being inexpensive and easy to make; pier foundations are free-standing concrete columns usually numbering four or six, one at each corner of an 8' x 40' container and often with additional support at each side of the center.

  o slab/raft foundation - as the name suggests this foundation is a slab of concrete that supports the entirety of the containers and also extends on each side of the border by two feet. This type of foundation is ideal for providing a stable and even surface to lay your container home. However, due to the amount of material needed as well as the work necessary to construct it, this foundation is more costly than other types.

- ○ pile foundation - piles are steel tubes that are driven into the ground to create a foundation primarily in situations where the soil is not dense enough to support a pier foundation.

- ○ strip/trims foundation - a mix between a slab and pier foundation that forms a border around the container when placed. Strip foundations provide a similar level of stability as a slab foundation but with less material and labor required to build.

- Place the containers - during the planning phase, a decision would have been made as to the orientation of the container, factoring in all the elements such as the views the property offers, the direction of the sunrise and sunset, and the direction of the daylight, and airflow. During the architectural planning stage of the project, an architect will include the layout of plumbing as well as electrical, HVAC, and fasteners to secure the container to the foundation. This information provides a guide to the contractor when the foundation and container are being placed that ensures that all these infrastructures are properly placed as efficiently as possible.

- Replace or treat container flooring - shipping containers are treated with chemicals that repel pests and rodents as they often transport goods that attract them. These chemicals are not safe for prolonged human exposure; therefore, it is critical that the wooden flooring in shipping containers be treated or removed altogether before it can become habitable.

- Cut out and reinforce windows and doors - shipping containers are sealed boxes, only accessible through a set of panel doors 8 feet wide on one end. Therefore, windows and doors must be cut out for additional access as well as to facilitate natural ventilation and lighting. Cutting windows and doors out of the frame will weaken the integrity of the structure and therefore, reinforcement of the windows and doors will become necessary to strengthen the frame of the container. The reinforcement can be achieved by welding steel frames on the border of the windows and doors.

- Framing for insulation - Containers are made of metal which is a thermal conductor that carries energy from one side to the other; this does not offer any protection from extreme heat or cold climates. Insulation is required to provide a barrier between the steel frame of the container and the living area. The framing for insulation is made of plyboard, primarily 2" x 2" or 2" x 4" and serves as a case for the insulation material. The framing should not only cover the walls but the ceiling and floor. The majority of the heat or cold will radiate from the ceiling; therefore, additional thermal protection may be necessary to add an extra layer of heat or cold protection.

- Install electrical, plumbing, and HVAC - before the insulation is put in, wires have to be put in for electrical sockets, light switches, etc., and pipes for the plumbing and the HVAC system. The building permit will likely stipulate that this process be completed by a licensed plumber and electrician in order to meet the building code.

- Install insulation - the climate of the area where the house is being built as well as the cost will determine the type of insulation that is best suited. The most commonly used types of insulation materials are as follows:

  o Foam insulation - this insulation material is made of varying types of plastics, usually polystyrene, polyisocyanurate, or polyurethane. The types of foam insulation are loose-fill, spray-on foam, and foam boards.

  o Fiberglass insulation - made of micro glass fibers that have been spun or blown into a board, loose-fill, rolls, or batts insulation. Fiberglass insulation utilizes recycled glass, and that adds to its appeal despite requiring precautionary measures when being used due to its propensity to irritate the skin and lungs.

- Cellulose insulation - made of recycled paper that has been shredded into tiny pieces and converted into a thread-like state; this allows it to be loose-fill and able to fit tightly into the cavities of a building, thus inhibiting airflow.

- Mineral wool insulation - both rock wool and slag wool fall under the category of mineral wool. Rock wool is made of natural minerals such as basalt and diabase, while slag wool is the byproduct of waste molten metal.

- Natural fibers insulation - natural fibers such as sheep wool, cotton straw, as well as hemp can be transformed into insulation material. These materials, however, require insect, fire, and moisture resistant treatment in order to be an ideal option. Natural fibers are typically available in the form of panels or batts.

- Denim insulation - a type of natural fiber insulation made from recycled denim or post-industrial denim cotton, typically coming in the form of batts. This type of insulation is ideal as it offers improved air quality and is more sustainable. It, however, requires treatment in order to be mold, fire, and pest resistant.

- Install plywood wall covering - this is optional and dependent on the required building codes that govern the area. Adding plywood over the insulation material will add an extra layer to secure the drywall to the frame of the interior wall.

- Framing and partitions - drywall partitions are ideal for creating partitions that separate rooms; it provides a clean, smooth texture that handles paint well.

- Install ceilings - the ceiling typically comprises the same materials as the wall: framing, insulation, plywood, and drywall with the wiring for lighting within the framing.

- Install floors – the original flooring from the shipping container as the material for the floor of the house is often chosen. After the wooden flooring has been removed and treated for chemicals, it is then polished; this makes a great option that looks rustic. There are also numerous other options such as floorboards, tiles, or carpet.

- Install windows and doors - to maintain the structure of the container, the number of cutouts to make windows and doors will likely have to be kept at a minimum; therefore, the space created for windows and doors will need to be utilized to its full potential, allowing the maximum amount of light and ventilation possible. The purpose that a room serves also determines the type of window or door that is appropriate for use; in a room that is used to host or serves as a common living space, an open and easily accessible setup will usually be most suitable. For areas in the house that require privacy, such as bedrooms and bathrooms, when selecting windows and doors, a less open choice is ideal. Glass sliding doors and windows are a great option to make the container home feel larger.

- Build and install storage space - in the drawing stage of the architectural plans, areas throughout the house that are ideal for storage spaces should be identified, and a design of how best it can be utilized included in the construction plans. Storage spaces such as cabinets can be built on-site, or they may be purchased at a hardware store; storage constructed on-site is built for the specific dimensions of the available space, so it is easier to create the ideal fit. The two main areas that require storage space to be built or installed are the kitchen and bedrooms. Storage for the kitchen includes cabinets, drawers, racks, counters, and shelves. Storage for bedrooms allows more ingenuity as storage beyond the conventional walk-in, or reach-in closet and wardrobe can be utilized. Ideas such as storage benches and under-bed storage are worth considering.

- Install outdoor siding - the grooves in the side of a shipping container have a visual appeal that's caused many homeowners to opt to leave it bare. Some persons have gone a step further and left the original paint untouched, although this is not always practical due to the wear suffered while transporting freight or while being modified for a container home. The process of getting the outer walls ready to install siding is the same as preparing the inner walls for drywall; framing is installed using 2" x 2" and 2" x 4". At this stage, an extra layer of insulation may be installed on the outer wall if you wish, and plywood is then placed on the frame; this will enable the use of any of the varied types of sidings. There are different styles, textures, materials, and sizes of siding. The following is a list of the frequently used types:

  - seamless steel siding

  - board and batten

  - vinyl siding

  - corrugated metals

- aluminum siding

- composite wood siding

- stucco siding

- stone veneer siding

- cement fiber siding

- wood clapboard siding

- brick veneer siding

- cedar shingle siding

- Roof installation - A shipping container that is in good condition will have a waterproof roof even after being modified for windows and doors and no longer being airtight. Despite its ability to withstand water damage, precautions should be taken to safeguard against corrosion in the future, as your shipping container home is a long-term investment. The least intrusive roofing option is using the container roof rather than constructing a new roof whose sole purpose is shading the container. Rather an effective method is the use of a waterproofing membrane such as a liquid rubber spray; the rubber adheres to the metal providing a layer of protection. There are also unique types of roofing such as a living roof, which can help to insulate the container home further while providing a green aesthetic.

Projected Budget

Construction is by far the widest spanning and most costly aspect of building a shipping container home. Hiring a workforce and purchasing materials will account for more of the budget than all the other expenses. Despite the expense, a shipping container costs a lot less to construct than a traditional brick and mortar home. In addition, most shipping container homes are DIY projects that only require licensed professionals for specific tasks that require verification such as the installation of electrical wiring and plumbing.

There are a few more upsides to a shipping container home that will result in savings that would not have been available with a traditional build. Primarily, not having to construct a frame from the ground up, which would require a vast amount of material and workforce is a big saving.

With shipping container homes, the materials used for the construction are typically standard and may only vary in amount based on size, therefore, it is plausible to create a list beforehand of what will be needed and a likely cost. The definitive numbers however will not be attained until a full architectural draft has analyzed the entire project in-depth. In addition, with the recent inflation seen in the prices of building materials, it can be hard to reach an accurate estimate. For that reason, it's always a good idea to have a little extra in your budget than you originally estimate will be necessary.

A basic rundown of the different aspects that should be expected during the construction process is as follows: excavation of the land, building the foundation for container placement, framing of the inside walls, laying of electrical wiring, laying of pipes for plumbing, insulation, an HVAC system, windows and doors, drywall installation, outdoor sidings (optional), roofing, floors, painting.

As is the case with all goods and services, there are variances in prices; the prices in one area might be lower or higher in another. Therefore, these estimated prices should only be used as a ballpark figure and not the amount that is used to formulate an actual budget. With everything taken into account for the construction of a house in the United States, the national average per square foot is $150; for a home that is approximately 2,000 square feet, the total cost of construction is on average $250,000 to $300,000 but may fluctuate based on the simplicity or complexity of the design.

Chapter 5: The Future of Shipping Container Homes

The United States real estate market has seen a shortage of homes available for sale in recent times. To fill this void, innovative approaches need to be taken. One solution is the creation of large-scale real estate developments. Shipping container homes on a large-scale development is currently an untapped market capable of providing many social and economic benefits. Entire communities can be developed using shipping containers as the primary building material, which would reduce the cost as well as the impact on the environment by using less raw material to create the base of the house. These savings could then be passed on to the eventual purchaser of the house resulting in an affordable housing solution.

In addition to the lessening of the environmental impact of a major real estate project by repurposing an otherwise wasted commodity, shipping container homes have the potential to create a sense of community.

Charity organizations that build low-income houses may also take advantage of this low-cost option. Currently, there is a homelessness crisis across cities in the United States, and solutions are being explored. Building single-container homes seems an obvious solution. One 40-foot container has the capacity to contain two bedrooms, a kitchen, and a bathroom; this could easily facilitate a small family.

With a current push for more renewable and sustainable practices in the areas of food, transport, and manufacturing, it makes sense that housing will follow suit. Most shipping containers are only used once, typically to transport goods from China or another manufacturing hub, all across the world. For the most part, these containers are perfectly usable, yet will either sit on a lot, wasting space, or they will be destroyed using expensive and unsustainable methods. Combine these facts with the ever-increasing cost of lumber, and the solution seems simple. These containers could be repurposed as building materials, saving people money while simultaneously providing a more sustainable and green way of providing people with housing.

Shipping container homes can be as simple or extravagant as you like. They range from simple, single-container structures, all the way up to multi-level mansions complete with shipping-container swimming pools! The container home revolution is still only in its early stages, but as it gains more momentum, there's no telling just how widely used this type of housing may become!

Conclusion

Kudos on taking the time and placing effort in educating yourself on a potentially life-changing opportunity. Let's assume you've decided to proceed with building a shipping container home. The reason that helped you determine that this is the ideal path for your journey to homeownership may be personal, financial, psychological, or a combination. The benefits they offer are innumerable and will likely leave you with a sense of accomplishment after making this decision.

There are several misconceptions regarding shipping container homes that often cause a prospective homeowner to become hesitant when deciding to build a container home. This book has addressed those misgivings, however a recap and reaffirmation of the benefits of a container home should serve as a fitting conclusion.

The most prevalent misunderstanding most persons have of container homes is the notion that it has to be a small narrow space only eight feet wide. This belief is detrimental because it may influence a person to design and construct a home that does not align with their desires. The ideal size shipping container home is a matter of personal preference, needs of the occupants, and available capital. If your choice is a large home, shipping containers can facilitate this decision with a multitude of design options.

A positive feature of shipping containers that makes them ideal for construction is that they are built to a standard dimension with a frame that can withstand up to 28 tons. The frame may also be reinforced to improve structural stability even further. As a result, there are few restrictions in regard to the size of houses that containers can be used to construct. Containers may be stacked on each other to form multiple stories. They may also be aligned on either side of a bridge which creates an open plan layout, or you could have four containers stacked and aligned, creating 1,284 square feet of space. The possible ways in which containers may be assembled to create a unique and functional home are endless and can be likened to building with Lego blocks.

Another point of concern regarding shipping container homes for many is how well they hold up in extreme climate situations. This is a valid concern as shipping containers are metallic boxes that are conductors of the external temperature. Whether a warm or cold temperature, it will radiate on the inside of the container. There is, however, a proven resolution for this: installing insulation and an HVAC system. When insulation is installed correctly and with sufficient thickness, it solves the conductivity issues shipping containers have. Coupled with an HVAC system, perfect temperature control indoors is easily achieved, despite the external temperature.

Admittedly some states have not yet established a process for approving the construction of container homes. This is, however, a minor impediment, and approval can be sought and acquired given that a carefully outlined architectural draft adheres to the state's building codes and zoning laws. Requests may also be submitted for special accommodations from the local permitting office.

Shipping container homes are increasing in popularity and inspiring new design concepts with each new home that is built. When constructed in accordance with the building codes tailored to the specific climate and variances in the weather for the area it is being built in, shipping container homes will stand the test of time and provide a dwelling that lasts a lifetime.

The amount of comfort and added features are only limited by the owner's thought and effort. Any addition that can be included when building a traditional brick-and-mortar house may also be added to your shipping container home. Not only are you able to have access to all the amenities you would with a traditional home, but due to their low carbon footprint, shipping containers have proven to be an ideal option for building in a natural environment. The material used in the construction of shipping container homes may be described as minimalist as its primarily lightweight plywood, lumber, and drywall.

Purchasing a property in a rural area will likely result in a much lower cost; this in most circumstances allows homeowners to purchase larger lots or multiple lots, which in turn enables additional developments on the property, potentially of multiple different container dwellings. This might mean you have a container home office separate to your main house, or perhaps you have multiple container homes strewn across your property that can earn you income on Airbnb.

Regardless of the decisions you will eventually make regarding the specifics for your shipping container home, such as size, location, layout, and design, building a shipping container home of your very own is a rewarding and worthwhile endeavor.

References

Abraham, Rachel. How Much Does It Cost to Build a House? Forbes Advisor, 18 June 2021, www.forbes.com/advisor/home-improvement/cost-to-build-a-house/

Are Container Homes Sustainable? We Weigh The Considerations - Attainable Home. (2021, December 10). https://www.attainablehome.com/are-container-homes-sustainable/#:~:text=The%20process%20of%20melting%20a

A Brief History of the Shipping Container. (n.d.). The Maritime Executive. https://www.maritime-executive.com/editorials/a-brief-history-of-the-shipping-container

Breaking down the Principles of Design (with Infographic). Toptal Design Blog. www.toptal.com/designers/gui/principles-of-design-infographic#:~:text=What%20are%20basic%20design%20principles

Building Permits. Investopedia. 2019. www.investopedia.com/terms/b/building-permits.asp

Choosing the Exterior Siding That Fits with Your Home Style. The Spruce. www.thespruce.com/exterior-siding-options-for-your-house-177587

Concept Architectural Design. Designingbuildings.co.uk

Container homes vs tiny homes Inspiration & Advice. (n.d.).https://www.refreshrenovations.co.nz/articles/container-homes-vs-tiny-homes

Containerization. (2022, June 18). Wikipedia. https://en.wikipedia.org/wiki/Containerization#Empty_containers

Creditor. Wikipedia, 18 Sept. 2020. en.wikipedia.org/wiki/Creditor

DAYLIGHT & ARCHITECTURE. n.d. Www.daylightandarchitecture.com, www.daylightandarchitecture.com/importance-of-windows-for-environmental-surfing/?consent=none&ref-original=https%3A%2F%2Fwww.google.com%2F

Design Principles. Www.designingbuildings.co.uk.
  www.designingbuildings.co.uk/wiki/Design_principles

Definition of Community | Dictionary.com. Www.dictionary.com, 2019.
  www.dictionary.com/browse/community

Development, M. (n.d.). 10 Tips for Choosing The Right Size Home.
  https://www.maltadevelopment.com/blog/choosing-right-size-
  home

Elements of Design. InVision. www.invisionapp.com/defined/elements-of-
  design

Litvak, Eugene. Council Post: Real Estate Development 101: The Myths, the
  Realities and How to Get Started. Forbes.
  www.forbes.com/sites/forbesrealestatecouncil/2021/07/29/real-
  estate-development-101-the-myths-the-realities-and-how-to-get-
  started/?sh=797783ed31f8

Feasibility Studies for Construction Projects. Designingbuildings.co.uk,
  2011.
  www.designingbuildings.co.uk/wiki/Feasibility_studies_for_constr
  uction_projects.InVision

Foundation Design for Shipping Container Homes. AMERICAN
  GEOSERVICES. americangeoservices.com/foundation-design-for-
  shipping-container-
  homes.html#:~:text=The%20four%20main%20foundation%20type
  s

How Much an Acre of Land Costs in Each State – Zippia.
  www.zippia.com/advice/acre-land-costs-each-state/

How Much Does a Used Shipping Container Cost. 1 June 2021.
  www.containeraddict.com/how-much-does-a-used-shipping-
  container-cost/

How Much Does It Cost to Hire an Architect? Angi, 23 Sept. 2011.
  www.angi.com/articles/how-much-does-architect-cost.htm

HOW to BUILD a SHIPPING CONTAINER HOUSE | STEP by STEP
  GUIDE. Www.youtube.com,
  www.youtube.com/watch?v=SEg68Pi_v1U

How to Choose the Right Windows and Doors for Your Project. HighQ
Windows & Doors, 13 Oct. 2016. www.highqdev.ca/blog/choose-
right-windows-doors-project/

How to Finance a Real Estate Development Project. GowerCrowd.
gowercrowd.com/real-estate-syndication/finance-development

Hwang, Billy. Should Public Infrastructure Be Delivered by Private
Developers? Medium, 8 Nov. 2018.
medium.com/@mr.mobillyty/should-public-infrastructure-be-
delivered-by-private-developers-4efb7d4fba79

Interior Design Basics for Each Room of Your House. The Spruce, 2018.
www.thespruce.com/decorating-101-interior-design-basics-4102142

Interior Design Styles 101: The Ultimate Guide to Defining Decorating Styles
in 2020. Decorilla Online Interior Design, 19 Mar. 2020.
www.decorilla.com/online-decorating/interior-design-styles-101/

Intermodal container. (2022, July 16). Wikipedia.
https://en.wikipedia.org/wiki/Intermodal_container#Repurposing

Jacobson, Michael. Why Are the Days Longer in Summer and Shorter in
Winter? Press & Sun-Bulletin, 4 May 2018.
www.pressconnects.com/story/news/local/2018/05/04/ask-
scientist-why-days-longer-summer-and-shorter-
winter/580359002/

Land Development. Wikipedia. 5 Dec. 2020.
en.wikipedia.org/wiki/Land_development

Lloyd, Lauren. How Much Does an Interior Designer Cost? Forbes Advisor.
23 Sept. 2021. www.forbes.com/advisor/home-improvement/cost-
to-hire-interior-
designer/#:~:text=Compare%20Quotes%20From%20Top%2Drated
%20Interior%20Decorators&text=Most%20interior%20designers%
20charge%20for

Learn about the Cost of Projects in the Home Design & Decor Category.
Www.homeadvisor.com, www.homeadvisor.com/cost/home-
design-and-decor/

Learn How Much It Costs to Hire an Architect. Homeadvisor.com 2019.
www.homeadvisor.com/cost/architects-and-engineers/hire-an-architect/

Modular Homes: Pros and Cons, Cost, and Buying Guide. (2015, November
13). MYMOVE. https://www.mymove.com/home-inspiration/trends/basic-facts-about-modular-homes/#:~:text=A%20modular%20home%20is%20one

NAHB: Typical American Subdivisions. Www.nahbclassic.org.
www.nahbclassic.org/generic.aspx?genericContentID=235108&fro
mGSA=1

9 Types of Construction Permits. Your Own Architect. 9 Aug. 2020.
www.yourownarchitect.com/9-types-of-construction-permits/#:~:text=The%20types%20of%20construction%20permits

People Are Turning Shipping Containers Into Tiny Homes. Here Are the
Pros and Cons. (2021, February 25). Time.
https://time.com/nextadvisor/mortgages/shipping-container-tiny-homes-new-norm/

Real Estate Development | Article and Definition of Real Estate
Development by Crepedia. Www.crepedia.com.
www.crepedia.com/dictionary/definitions/real-estate-development/#:~:text=A%20project%20under%20construction%2
0or

Real Estate Development Model - Overview, Guide, and Steps. Corporate
Finance Institute.
corporatefinanceinstitute.com/resources/knowledge/modeling/real
-estate-development-model/

Real Estate Development. Wikipedia, Wikimedia Foundation. 13 Mar. 2019.
en.wikipedia.org/wiki/Real_estate_development

SECURE. (2020, June 8). How Shipping Container Architecture Has
Evolved Over the Years. Secure Container Solutions.
https://www.securecontainer.ca/shipping-container-architecture-evolved-years/

ShelterMode. How to Build a Shipping Container Home in 7 Simple Steps. YouTube. 17 Jan. 2021. www.youtube.com/watch?v=NS-thd1A-C0

Shipping container. (2022, May 5). Wikipedia. https://en.wikipedia.org/wiki/Shipping_container#Re-use

Shipping container architecture. (2019, November 21). Wikipedia. https://en.wikipedia.org/wiki/Shipping_container_architecture

6 Steps to Building a Shipping Container Home. Storagecontainer. storagecontainer.com/blog/6-steps-to-building-a-shipping-container-home/

Subdivision (Land). Wikipedia. 31 Oct. 2021. en.wikipedia.org/wiki/Subdivision_(land)

Temperature and Heat -- Thermal Conduction. Www.pa.uky.edu. www.pa.uky.edu/sciworks/courses/heat/cond4.htm

10 Different Types of Furniture Styles (2022 Photo Guide). Home Stratosphere, 4 Jan. Staff, Author Homestratosphere's Editorial, and Writers. 2020. www.homestratosphere.com/types-of-furniture-styles/

The Cost of Furnishing an Apartment | a Detailed Guide to Furnish a Home. Furnishr. 22 Sept. 2020, furnishr.com/blog/cost-furnishing-apartment/

The Box That Changed Asia and the World. (n.d.). Forbes. https://www.forbes.com/global/2006/0313/030.html?sh=4a4944a04cd7

The 5 Steps of Design, or How Architects Do What They Do - Architizer Journal. Journal. architizer.com/blog/inspiration/industry/the-5-steps-of-design-or-how-architects-do-what-they-do/

Study.com study.com/learn/lesson/type-of-land-use-overview-examples.html

The Great Recession's Impact on the Housing Market. (n.d.). Investopedia. https://www.investopedia.com/investing/great-recessions-impact-housing-market/#:~:text=A%20combination%20of%20rising%20home

The Ultimate Guide to Types of Insulation. Cielo Breez. 27 Aug. 2021.
www.cielowigle.com/blog/types-of-insulation/

35 Different Types of Houses (with Photos). Home Stratosphere, About the
Homestratosphere Editorial Staff & Writers. Home Stratosphere. 22
Aug. 2019. www.homestratosphere.com/types-of-houses/

35 Home Storage Ideas (Room-By-Room). Home Stratosphere. 19 Mar.
2019. www.homestratosphere.com/home-storage-ideas/

Tiny-house movement. (2022, July 6). Wikipedia.
https://en.wikipedia.org/wiki/Tiny-
house_movement#Environmentally_conscious_design

Walker, Andy. "Natural Ventilation | WBDG - Whole Building Design
Guide." Wbdg.org. 2016. www.wbdg.org/resources/natural-
ventilation

Waterproofing Membrane for Metal Roof - Shipping Containers. YouTube.
www.youtube.com/watch?v=xDEDQ_sVpPk

Who was the first person to build a shipping container home? 2018, April 14.
https://www.cargohome.com/2018/04/14/who-was-the-first-
person-to-build-a-shipping-container-home/

Window Orientation and Shading. Www.fsec.ucf.edu.
www.fsec.ucf.edu/en/consumer/buildings/homes/windows/shadin
g.htm

Wikipedia Contributors. Civil Engineer. Wikipedia, Wikimedia Foundation.
24 Apr. 2019, en.wikipedia.org/wiki/Civil_engineer

Wikipedia Contributors. (2019, December 12). Weathering steel. Wikipedia.
Wikimedia Foundation.
https://en.wikipedia.org/wiki/Weathering_steel

US, B/A Stores-Furniture. Furniture Styles: The Most Popular Types.
Medium. 20 May 2016. medium.com/@bastores/furniture-styles-
the-most-popular-types-5bde68cf10e2

www.ingramcontent.com/pod-product-compliance
Lightning Source LLC
Chambersburg PA
CBHW070937120626
46546CB00004B/1441